TAO TE CHING

TAO TE CHING

LAO TZU

This edition published in 2025 by Arcturus Publishing Limited
26/27 Bickels Yard, 151–153 Bermondsey Street,
London SE1 3HA

AD012315UK

Printed in China

CONTENTS

INTRODUCTION

The *Tao Te Ching* is a timeless guide to the art of living and full of ancient wisdom. However, in common with other works that come from ancient China, such as *The Art of War*, there are many concepts and ideas in this book that are universal truths that have significance for modern times. Most significantly perhaps, at a time when arguments rage about the continuing use of fossil fuels – a proven cause of climate change – is Lao Tzu's insistence that we should live in harmony with nature by aligning ourselves with its laws and the order of things that have made our planet so beautiful for so long. Despite his 2,500-year-old advice, it is hard not to agree that we are further away than ever from nature's way.

Granted, fossil fuels have been a success for many, having driven the rise of capitalism as an economic system, particularly in the West, for more than 500 years. But now we seem to have exceeded nature's limits in terms of population, energy usage, raw materials and the pollution we produce. Unless we change course in time, the walls will surely come tumbling down.

Out of Control

Other recurring themes in these texts include the need for us to find balance, a major component of the natural cycle. In today's fast-moving, information-led, consumerist world, it is hard not to feel overwhelmed and out of control. Without balance in our thinking, we can easily take wrong turns and make the wrong decisions. For Lao Tzu, *wu wei* (or 'non-action') is the answer, taking actions that go with the flow of circumstances and help align us with what is actually happening and work in harmony with the natural cycle of things. To help us understand this concept, Lao Tzu explains that seeming opposites – dark and light, soft and hard, good and evil – are actually two sides of the same coin, as one cannot exist without the other. Understanding this paradox will help us find balance in our logic. He also points out the importance of self-awareness in achieving emotional balance, which will help you develop self-discipline and ensure you make your own decisions rather than being overly influenced by others. Lao Tzu promotes the notion of inner peace, which you can achieve through stillness, being present and letting go of the ego and desire. The management of a sensible work-life balance can play a huge part in this.

Practise mindfulness meditation

In the introduction for his own translation of this classic book, Victor Mair, Professor of Chinese Language and Literature at the University of Pennsylvania, explains that Taoism was heavily influenced by the Yogic tradition of southern Asia, which helps explain why so much of Lao Tzu's advice involves breathing exercises, daily quiet time and some form of meditation rather than simple, practical advice.

Finding time to sit quietly and comfortably and detach yourself from the hubbub of daily life allows you to think more clearly. Breathing and focusing on the present moment in mindfulness meditation helps us empty our thoughts, let go of pressing desires and appreciate the simplicity of the moment. The compilation of a 'grateful list' can help us find contentment in what we have rather than what we are told that we need.

Practical advice

Lao Tzu offers some practical advice too, on relationships, conflict resolution and leadership. He points out that investing in our relationships and our shared experiences will give us greater inner peace than any material possessions. He explains how avoiding judgement, developing compassion and sharing our own knowledge with others will help our own well-being as well as theirs. He points out the uselessness of violence and stresses instead the advantages of leadership through listening, service to others, trust, integrity and non-violent conflict resolution, rather than the self-important, ego-driven actions of ambitious leaders that are so common in our world today.

Despite the fact that each of us shares our planet with some seven million other human beings, we must all play our part in its history. Look inside yourself, find the inner you and love the world as much as you love yourself. If we all did that, it would be a better world for everyone.

A guide to the cards

Included in this beautifully packaged edition of the *Tao Te Ching* is a set of 52 cards, each of which features a specially selected quote from Lao Tzu's text on one side and advice and an explanation on the other. On the side containing the quote, you will see the number of the card on the left and the number of the verse in the *Tao Te Ching* it is taken from on the right. Despite being 2,500 years old, the advice contained will have relevance for your life today, most importantly on you as a person, your self-knowledge, your attitude to others, your fears and how you contribute to the planet on which you live.

Much of this advice advocates taking a moment or two each day for reflection, so find a quiet, comfortable and warm place somewhere in your home that you can use regularly for the purpose. Shuffle the cards, take the top card from the pile and read the quoted text. Turn the card over and consider the advice. Place the card on the stand included in the pack, place it where you can see it and think about what he says and how it might relate to you. Breathe deeply, let your thoughts wander, consider situations in your life where this advice could be helpful. Taking a moment out of your busy day to do this will calm your mind, empty it of the everyday chaos of life, re-find your balance and make space in your brain for new, more focused thoughts. When relaxed, our brains go into alpha-wave mode, when we come up with our most creative ideas. However you do it, you will emerge refreshed from a session like this, perhaps with new ideas, new determinations and possibly even a solution to a problem that is bothering you.

TAO TE CHING

Translated by
John H. McDonald

1

The tao that can be described
is not the eternal Tao.
The name that can be spoken
is not the eternal Name.

The nameless is the boundary of Heaven and Earth.
The named is the mother of creation.

Freed from desire, you can see the hidden mystery.
By having desire, you can only see what is visibly real.

Yet mystery and reality
emerge from the same source.
This source is called darkness.

Darkness born from darkness.
The beginning of all understanding.

2

When people see things as beautiful,
ugliness is created.
When people see things as good,
evil is created.

Being and non-being produce each other.
Difficult and easy complement each other.
Long and short define each other.
High and low oppose each other.
Fore and aft follow each other.
Therefore the Master
can act without doing anything
and teach without saying a word.
Things come her way and she does not stop them;
things leave and she lets them go.
She has without possessing,
and acts without any expectations.
When her work is done, she takes no credit.
That is why it will last forever.

3

If you over-esteem talented individuals,
people will become overly competitive.
If you overvalue possessions,
people will begin to steal.

Do not display your treasures
or people will become envious.

The Master leads by
emptying people's minds,
filling their bellies,
weakening their ambitions,
and making them become strong.
Preferring simplicity and freedom from desires,
avoiding the pitfalls of knowledge and wrong action.

For those who practise not-doing,
everything will fall into place.

4

The Tao is like an empty container:
it can never be emptied and can never be filled.
Infinitely deep, it is the source of all things.
It dulls the sharp, unties the knotted,
shades the lighted, and unites all of creation with dust.

It is hidden but always present.
I don't know who gave birth to it.
It is older than the concept of God.

5

Heaven and Earth are impartial;
they treat all of creation as straw dogs.
The Master doesn't take sides;
she treats everyone like a straw dog.

The space between Heaven and Earth is like a bellows;
it is empty, yet has not lost its power.
The more it is used, the more it produces;
the more you talk of it, the less you comprehend.

It is better not to speak of things you do not understand.

6

The spirit of emptiness is immortal.
It is called the Great Mother
because it gives birth to Heaven and Earth.

It is like a vapour,
barely seen but always present.
Use it effortlessly.

7

The Tao of Heaven is eternal,
and the earth is long enduring.
Why are they long enduring?
They do not live for themselves;
thus they are present for all beings.

The Master puts herself last;
And finds herself in the place of authority.
She detaches herself from all things;
Therefore she is united with all things.
She gives no thought to self.
She is perfectly fulfilled.

8

The supreme good is like water,
which benefits all of creation
without trying to compete with it.
It gathers in unpopular places.
Thus it is like the Tao.

The location makes the dwelling good.
Depth of understanding makes the mind good.
A kind heart makes the giving good.
Integrity makes the government good.
Accomplishment makes your labours good.
Proper timing makes a decision good.

Only when there is no competition
will we all live in peace.

元配吳太孺人之位

9

It is easier to carry an empty cup
than one that is filled to the brim.

The sharper the knife
the easier it is to dull.
The more wealth you possess
the harder it is to protect.
Pride brings its own trouble.

When you have accomplished your goal
simply walk away.
This is the pathway to Heaven.

10

Nurture the darkness of your soul
until you become whole.
Can you do this and not fail?
Can you focus your life-breath until you become
supple as a newborn child?
While you cleanse your inner vision
will you be found without fault?
Can you love people and lead them
without forcing your will on them?
When Heaven gives and takes away
can you be content with the outcome?
When you understand all things
can you step back from your own understanding?

Giving birth and nourishing,
making without possessing,
expecting nothing in return.
To grow, yet not to control:
This is the mysterious virtue.

11

Thirty spokes are joined together in a wheel,
but it is the centre hole
that allows the wheel to function.

We mould clay into a pot,
but it is the emptiness inside
that makes the vessel useful.

We fashion wood for a house,
but it is the emptiness inside
that makes it liveable.

We work with the substantial,
but the emptiness is what we use.

12

Five colours blind the eye.
Five notes deafen the ear.
Five flavours make the palate go stale.
Too much activity deranges the mind.
Too much wealth causes crime.
The Master acts on what she feels and not what she sees.
She shuns the latter, and prefers to seek the former.

13

Success is as dangerous as failure,
and we are often our own worst enemy.

What does it mean that success is as dangerous as failure?
He who is superior is also someone's subordinate.
Receiving favour and losing it both cause alarm.
That is what is meant by success is as dangerous as failure.
What does it mean that we are often our own worst
enemy?
The reason I have an enemy is because I have 'self'.
If I no longer had a 'self', I would no longer have an
enemy.

Love the whole world as if it were your self;
then you will truly care for all things.

14

Look for it, and it can't be seen.
Listen for it, and it can't be heard.
Grasp for it, and it can't be caught.
These three cannot be further described,
so we treat them as The One.

Its highest is not bright.
Its depths are not dark.
Unending, unnameable, it returns to nothingness.
Formless forms, and imageless images,
subtle, beyond all understanding.

Approach it and you will not see a beginning;
follow it and there will be no end.
When we grasp the Tao of the ancient ones,
we can use it to direct our life today.
To know the ancient origin of Tao:
this is the beginning of wisdom.

15

The Sages of old were profound
and knew the ways of subtlety and discernment.
Their wisdom is beyond our comprehension.
Because their knowledge was so far superior
I can only give a poor description.

They were careful
as someone crossing a frozen stream in winter.
Alert as if surrounded on all sides by the enemy.
Courteous as a guest.
Fluid as melting ice.
Whole as an uncarved block of wood.
Receptive as a valley.
Turbid as muddied water.

Who can be still
until their mud settles
and the water is cleared by itself?
Can you remain tranquil until right action occurs by itself?

The Master doesn't seek fulfilment.
For only those who are not full are able to be used,
which brings the feeling of completeness.

16

If you can empty your mind of all thoughts
your heart will embrace the tranquility of peace.
Watch the workings of all of creation,
but contemplate their return to the source.

All creatures in the universe
return to the point where they began.
Returning to the source is tranquility
because we submit to Heaven's mandate.

Returning to Heaven's mandate is called being constant.
Knowing the constant is called 'enlightenment'.
Not knowing the constant is the source of evil deeds
because we have no roots.
By knowing the constant we can accept things as they are.
By accepting things as they are, we become impartial.
By being impartial, we become one with Heaven.
By being one with Heaven, we become one with Tao.
Being one with Tao, we are no longer concerned about
losing our life because we know the Tao is constant
and we are one with Tao.

17

The best leaders are those the people hardly know exist.
The next best is a leader who is loved and praised.
Next comes the one who is feared.
The worst one is the leader who is despised.

If you don't trust the people,
they will become untrustworthy.

The best leaders value their words, and use them
sparingly.
When the Master has accomplished her task,
the people say, 'Amazing:
we did it, all by ourselves!'

18

When the great Tao is abandoned,
charity and righteousness appear.
When intellectualism arises,
hypocrisy is close behind.

When there is strife in the family unit,
people talk about 'brotherly love'.

When the country falls into chaos,
politicians talk about 'patriotism'.

19

Forget about knowledge and wisdom,
and people will be a hundred times better off.
Throw away charity and righteousness,
and people will return to brotherly love.
Throw away profit and greed,
and there won't be any thieves.

These three are superficial and aren't enough
to keep us at the centre of the circle, so we must also:

Embrace simplicity.
Put others first.
Desire little.

20

Renounce knowledge and your problems will end.
What is the difference between yes and no?
What is the difference between good and evil?
Must you fear what others fear?
Nonsense, look how far you have missed the mark!

Other people are joyous,
as though they were at a spring festival.
I alone am unconcerned and expressionless,
like an infant before it has learned to smile.
Other people have more than they need;
I alone seem to possess nothing.
I am lost and drift about with no place to go.
I am like a fool, my mind is in chaos.

Ordinary people are bright;
I alone am dark.
Ordinary people are clever;
I alone am dull.
Ordinary people seem discriminating;
I alone am muddled and confused.
I drift on the waves on the ocean,
blown at the mercy of the wind.
Other people have their goals,
I alone am dull and uncouth.

I am different from ordinary people.
I nurse from the Great Mother's breasts.

21

The greatest virtue you can have
comes from following only the Tao;
which takes a form that is intangible and evasive.

Even though the Tao is intangible and evasive,
we are able to know it exists.
Intangible and evasive, yet it has a manifestation.
Secluded and dark, yet there is a vitality within it.
Its vitality is very genuine.
Within it we can find order.

Since the beginning of time, the Tao has always existed.
It is beyond existing and not existing.
How do I know where creation comes from?
I look inside myself and see it.

22

If you want to become whole,
first let yourself become broken.
If you want to become straight,
first let yourself become twisted.
If you want to become full,
first let yourself become empty.
If you want to become new,
first let yourself become old.
Those whose desires are few get them,
those whose desires are great go astray.

For this reason the Master embraces the Tao,
as an example for the world to follow.
Because she isn't self-centred,
people can see the light in her.
Because she does not boast of herself,
she becomes a shining example.
Because she does not glorify herself,
she becomes a person of merit.
Because she wants nothing from the world,
the world cannot overcome her.
When the ancient Masters said,
'If you want to become whole,
then first let yourself be broken,'
they weren't using empty words.
All who do this will be made complete.

23

Nature uses few words:
when the gale blows, it will not last long;
when it rains hard, it lasts but a little while;
What causes these to happen? Heaven and Earth.

Why do we humans go on endlessly about little
when nature does much in a little time?
If you open yourself to the Tao,
you and Tao become one.
If you open yourself to Virtue,
then you can become virtuous.
If you open yourself to loss,
then you will become lost.
If you open yourself to the Tao,
the Tao will eagerly welcome you.
If you open yourself to virtue,
virtue will become a part of you.
If you open yourself to loss,
the lost are glad to see you.

When you do not trust people,
people will become untrustworthy.

24

Those who stand on tiptoes
do not stand firmly.
Those who rush ahead
don't get very far.
Those who try to outshine others
dim their own light.
Those who call themselves righteous
can't know how wrong they are.
Those who boast of their accomplishments
diminish the things they have done.

Compared to the Tao, these actions are unworthy.
If we are to follow the Tao, we must not do these things.

25

Before the universe was born
there was something in the chaos of the heavens.
It stands alone and empty,
solitary and unchanging.
It is ever present and secure.
It may be regarded as the Mother of the universe.
Because I do not know its name,
I call it the Tao.
If forced to give it a name,
I would call it 'Great'.

Because it is Great means it is everywhere.
Being everywhere means it is eternal.
Being eternal means everything returns to it.

Tao is great.
Heaven is great.
Earth is great.
Humanity is great.
Within the universe, these are the four great things.

Humanity follows the earth.
Earth follows Heaven.
Heaven follows the Tao.
The Tao follows only itself.

26

Heaviness is the basis of lightness.
Stillness is the standard of activity.

Thus the Master travels all day
without ever leaving her wagon.
Even though she has much to see,
she is at peace in her indifference.

Why should the lord of a thousand chariots
be amused at the foolishness of the world?
If you abandon yourself to foolishness,
you lose touch with your beginnings.
If you let yourself become distracted,
you will lose the basis of your power.

27

A good traveller leaves no tracks,
and a skilful speaker is well rehearsed.
A good bookkeeper has an excellent memory,
and a well-made door is easy to open and needs no locks.
A good knot needs no rope and it can not come undone.

Thus the Master is willing to help everyone,
and doesn't know the meaning of rejection.
She is there to help all of creation,
and doesn't abandon even the smallest creature.
This is called embracing the light.

What is a good person but a bad person's teacher?
What is a bad person but raw material for his teacher?
If you fail to honour your teacher or fail to enjoy your
student,
you will become deluded no matter how smart you are.
It is the secret of prime importance.

28

Know the masculine,
but keep to the feminine:
and become a watershed to the world.
If you embrace the world,
the Tao will never leave you
and you become as a little child.

Know the white,
yet keep to the black:
be a model for the world.
If you are a model for the world,
the Tao inside you will strengthen
and you will return whole to your eternal beginning.

Know the honourable,
but do not shun the disgraced:
embracing the world as it is.
If you embrace the world with compassion,
then your virtue will return you to the
Uncarved Block.

The block of wood is carved into utensils
by carving void into the wood.
The Master uses the utensils, yet prefers to keep to the block
because of its limitless possibilities.
Great works do not involve discarding substance.

29

Do you want to rule the world and control it?
I don't think it can ever be done.

The world is a sacred vessel
and it can not be controlled.
You will only make it worse if you try.
It may slip through your fingers and disappear.

Some are meant to lead,
and others are meant to follow;
Some must always strain,
and others have an easy time;
Some are naturally big and strong,
and others will always be small;
Some will be protected and nurtured,
and others will meet with destruction.

The Master accepts things as they are,
and out of compassion avoids extravagance,
excess and the extremes.

30

Those who lead people by following the Tao
don't use weapons to enforce their will.
Using force always leads to unseen troubles.

In the places where armies march,
thorns and briars bloom and grow.
After armies take to war,
bad years must always follow.
The skilful commander
strikes a decisive blow then stops.
When victory is won over the enemy through war
it is not a thing of great pride.
When the battle is over,
arrogance is the new enemy.
War can result when no other alternative is given,
so the one who overcomes an enemy should not dominate
    them.
The strong are always weakened with time.

This is not the way of the Tao.
That which is not of the Tao will soon end.

31

Weapons are the bearers of bad news;
all people should detest them.

The wise man values the left side,
and in time of war he values the right.
Weapons are meant for destruction,
and thus are avoided by the wise.
Only as a last resort
will a wise person use a deadly weapon.
If peace is her true objective
how can she rejoice in the victory of war?
Those who rejoice in victory
delight in the slaughter of humanity.
Those who resort to violence
will never bring peace to the world.

The left side is a place of honour on happy occasions.
The right side is reserved for mourning at a funeral.
When the lieutenants take the left side to prepare for war,
the general should be on the right side,
because he knows the outcome will be death.
The death of many should be greeted with great sorrow,
and the victory celebration should honour those who have
died.

32

The Tao is nameless and unchanging.
Although it appears insignificant,
nothing in the world can contain it.

If a ruler abides by its principles,
then her people will willingly follow.
Heaven would then reign on earth,
like sweet rain falling on paradise.
People would have no need for laws,
because the law would be written on their hearts.

Naming is a necessity for order,
but naming can not order all things.
Naming often makes things impersonal,
so we should know when naming should end.
Knowing when to stop naming,
you can avoid the pitfall it brings.

All things end in the Tao
just as the small streams and the largest rivers
flow through valleys to the sea.

33

Those who know others are intelligent;
those who know themselves are truly wise.
Those who master others are strong;
those who master themselves have true power.

Those who know they have enough are truly wealthy.

Those who persist will reach their goal.

Those who keep their course have a strong will.
Those who embrace death will not perish,
but have life everlasting.

34

The great Tao flows unobstructed in every direction.
All things rely on it to conceive and be born,
and it does not deny even the smallest of creation.
When it has accomplished great wonders,
it does not claim them for itself.
It nourishes infinite worlds,
yet it doesn't seek to master the smallest creature.
Since it is without wants and desires,
it can be considered humble.
All of creation seeks it for refuge
yet it does not seek to master or control.
Because it does not seek greatness,
it is able to accomplish truly great things.

35

She who follows the way of the Tao
will draw the world to her steps.
She can go without fear of being injured,
because she has found peace and tranquility in her heart.

Where there is music and good food,
people will stop to enjoy it.
But words spoken of the Tao
seem to them boring and stale.
When looked at, there is nothing for them to see.
When listened for, there is nothing for them to hear.
Yet if they put it to use, it would never be exhausted.

36

If you want something to return to the source,
you must first allow it to spread out.
If you want something to weaken,
you must first allow it to become strong.
If you want something to be removed,
you must first allow it to flourish.
If you want to possess something,
you must first give it away.

This is called the subtle understanding
of how things are meant to be.

The soft and pliable overcomes the hard and inflexible.

Just as fish remain hidden in deep waters,
it is best to keep weapons out of sight.

37

The Tao never acts with force,
yet there is nothing that it cannot do.

If rulers could follow the way of the Tao,
then all of creation would willingly follow their example.
If selfish desires were to arise after their transformation,
I would erase them with the power of the Uncarved Block.

By the power of the Uncarved Block,
future generations would lose their selfish desires.
By losing their selfish desires,
the world would naturally settle into peace.

38

The highest good is not to seek to do good,
but to allow yourself to become it.
The ordinary person seeks to do good things,
and finds that they can not do them continually.

The Master does not force virtue on others,
thus she is able to accomplish her task.
The ordinary person who uses force,
will find that they accomplish nothing.

The kind person acts from the heart,
and accomplishes a multitude of things.
The righteous person acts out of pity,
yet leaves many things undone.
The moral person will act out of duty,
and when no one responds
will roll up his sleeves and use force.

When the Tao is forgotten, there is righteousness.
When righteousness is forgotten, there is morality.
When morality is forgotten, there is the law.
The law is the husk of faith,
and trust is the beginning of chaos.

Our basic understandings are not from the Tao
because they come from the depths of our mis-
understanding.
The master abides in the fruit and not in the husk.
She dwells in the Tao,
and not with the things that hide it.
This is how she increases in wisdom.

39

The masters of old attained unity with the Tao.
Heaven attained unity and became pure.
The earth attained unity and found peace.
The spirits attained unity so they could minister.
The valleys attained unity that they might be full.
Humanity attained unity that they might flourish.
Their leaders attained unity that they might set the example.
This is the power of unity.

Without unity, the sky becomes filthy.
Without unity, the earth becomes unstable.
Without unity, the spirits become unresponsive and disappear.
Without unity, the valleys become dry as a desert.
Without unity, humankind can't reproduce and becomes extinct.
Without unity, our leaders become corrupt and fall.

The great view the small as their source,
and the high take the low as their foundation.
Their greatest asset becomes their humility.
They speak of themselves as orphans and widows,
thus they truly seek humility.
Do not shine like the precious gem,
but be as dull as a common stone.

40

All movement returns to the Tao.
Weakness is how the Tao works.

All of creation is born from substance.
Substance is born of nothing-ness.

41

When a superior person hears of the Tao,
she diligently puts it into practice.
When an average person hears of the Tao,
he believes half of it, and doubts the other half.
When a foolish person hears of the Tao,
he laughs out loud at the very idea.
If he didn't laugh,
it wouldn't be the Tao.

Thus it is said:
The brightness of the Tao seems like darkness,
the advancement of the Tao seems like retreat,
the level path seems rough,
the superior path seems empty,
the pure seems to be tarnished,
and true virtue doesn't seem to be enough.
The virtue of caution seems like cowardice,
the pure seems to be polluted,
the true square seems to have no corners,
the best vessels take the most time to finish,
the greatest sounds cannot be heard,
and the greatest image has no form.

The Tao hides in the unnamed,
Yet it alone nourishes and completes all things.

42

The Tao gave birth to One.
The One gave birth to Two.
The Two gave birth to Three.
The Three gave birth to all of creation.

All things carry Yin
yet embrace Yang.
They blend their life breaths
in order to produce harmony.

People despise being orphaned, widowed and poor.
But the noble ones take these as their titles.
In losing, much is gained,
and, in gaining, much is lost.

What others teach I too will teach:
'The strong and violent will not die a natural death.'

43

That which offers no resistance,
overcomes the hardest substances.
That which offers no resistance
can enter where there is no space.

Few in the world can comprehend
the teaching without words,
or understand the value of non-action.

44

Which is more important, your honour or your life?
Which is more valuable, your possessions or your person?
Which is more destructive, success or failure?

Great love extracts a great cost
and true wealth requires greater loss.

Knowing when you have enough avoids dishonour,
and knowing when to stop will keep you from danger
and bring you a long, happy life.

45

The greatest accomplishments seem imperfect,
yet their usefulness is not diminished.
The greatest fullness seems empty,
yet it will be inexhaustible.

The greatest straightness seems crooked.
The most valued skill seems like clumsiness.
The greatest speech seems full of stammers.

Movement overcomes the cold,
and stillness overcomes the heat.
That which is pure and still is the universal ideal.

46

When the world follows the Tao,
horses run free to fertilize the fields.
When the world does not follow the Tao,
war horses are bred outside the cities.

There is no greater transgression
than condoning people's selfish desires,
no greater disaster than being discontent,
and no greater retribution than for greed.

Whoever knows contentment will be at peace forever.

47

Without opening your door,
you can know the whole world.
Without looking out of your window,
you can understand the way of the Tao.

The more knowledge you seek,
the less you will understand.

The Master understands without leaving,
sees clearly without looking,
accomplishes much without doing anything.

48

One who seeks knowledge learns something new every day.
One who seeks the Tao unlearns something new every day.
Less and less remains until you arrive at non-action.
When you arrive at non-action,
nothing will be left undone.

Mastery of the world is achieved
by letting things take their natural course.
You can not master the world by changing the natural way.

49

The Master has no mind of her own.
She understands the mind of the people.

Those who are good she treats as good.
Those who aren't good she also treats as good.
This is how she attains true goodness.

She trusts people who are trustworthy.
She also trusts people who aren't trustworthy.
This is how she gains true trust.

The Master's mind is shut off from the world.
Only for the sake of the people does she muddle her mind.
They look to her in anticipation. Yet she treats them all as
her children.

50

Those who leave the womb at birth
and those who enter their source at death,
of these; three out of ten celebrate life,
three out of ten celebrate death,
and three out of ten simply go from life to death.
What is the reason for this?
Because they are afraid of dying,
therefore they cannot live.

I have heard that those who celebrate life
walk safely among the wild animals.
When they go into battle, they remain unharmed.
The animals find no place to attack them
and the weapons are unable to harm them.
Why? Because they can find no place for death in them.

昔趙松雪作高岡鳴鳳圖後人傳之久矣
以訛傳訛將鳳鳥真蹟失矣今為仿之雖是
呂紀畫

定林寺圖
鍾山已在萬山深更過鍾山入定林穿
盡松杉行盡石一庵猶隔白雲岑
蓮巢居士恭壽作

51

The Tao gives birth to all of creation.
The virtue of Tao in nature nurtures them,
and their family gives them their form.
Their environment then shapes them into completion.
That is why every creature honours the Tao and its virtue.

No one tells them to honour the Tao and its virtue,
it happens all by itself.
So the Tao gives them birth,
and its virtue cultivates them,
cares for them,
nurtures them,
gives them a place of refuge and peace,
helps them to grow and shelters them.

It gives them life without wanting to possess them,
and cares for them expecting nothing in return.
It is their master, but it does not seek to dominate them.
This is called the dark and mysterious virtue.

52

The world had a beginning
which we call the Great Mother.
Once we have found the Mother,
we begin to know what Her children should be.

When we know we are the Mother's child,
we begin to guard the qualities of the Mother in us.
She will protect us from all danger
even if we lose our life.

Keep your mouth closed
and embrace a simple life,
and you will live care-free until the end of your days.
If you try to talk your way into a better life
there will be no end to your trouble.

To understand the small is called clarity.
Knowing how to yield is called strength.
To use your inner light for understanding
regardless of the danger
is called depending on the Constant.

53

If I understood only one thing,
I would want to use it to follow the Tao.
My only fear would be one of pride.
The Tao goes in the level places,
but people prefer to take the short cuts.

If too much time is spent cleaning the house
the land will become neglected and full of weeds,
and the granaries will soon become empty
because there is no one out working the fields.
To wear fancy clothes and ornaments,
to have your fill of food and drink
and to waste all of your money buying possessions
is called the crime of excess.
Oh, how these things go against the way of the Tao!

54

That which is well built
will never be torn down.
That which is well latched
can not slip away.
Those who do things well
will be honoured from generation to generation.

If this idea is cultivated in the individual,
then his virtue will become genuine.
If this idea is cultivated in your family,
then virtue in your family will be great.
If this idea is cultivated in your community,
then virtue will go a long way.
If this idea is cultivated in your country,
then virtue will be in many places.
If this idea is cultivated in the world,
then virtue will be with everyone.

Then observe the person for what the person does,
and observe the family for what it does,
and observe the community for what it does,
and observe the country for what it does,
and observe the world for what it does.
How do I know this saying is true?
I observe these things and see.

55

One who is filled with the Tao
is like a newborn child.
The infant is protected from
the stinging insects, wild beasts, and birds of prey.
Its bones are soft, its muscles are weak,
but its grip is firm and strong.
It doesn't know about the union
of male and female,
yet his penis can stand erect
because of the power of life within him.
It can cry all day and never become hoarse.
This is perfect harmony.

To understand harmony is to understand the Constant.
To know the Constant is to be called 'enlightened'.
To unnaturally try to extend life is not appropriate.
To try and alter the life-breath is unnatural.
The master understands that when something reaches its
prime
it will soon begin to decline.
Changing the natural is against the way of the Tao.
Those who do it will come to an early end.

56

Those who know do not talk.
Those who talk do not know.

Stop talking,
meditate in silence,
blunt your sharpness,
release your worries,
harmonize your inner light,
and become one with the dust.
Doing this is called the dark and mysterious identity.

Those who have achieved the mysterious identity
can not be approached, and they can not be alienated.
They can not be benefited nor harmed.
They can not be made noble nor to suffer disgrace.
This makes them the most noble of all under the heavens.

57

Govern your country with integrity,
Weapons of war can be used with great cunning,
but loyalty is only won by not-doing.
How do I know the way things are?
By these:

The more prohibitions you make,
the poorer people will be.
The more weapons you possess,
the greater the chaos in your country.
The more knowledge that is acquired,
the stranger the world will become.
The more laws that you make,
the greater the number of criminals.

Therefore the Master says:
I do nothing,
and people become good by themselves.
I seek peace,
and people take care of their own problems.
I do not meddle in their personal lives,
and the people become prosperous.
I let go of all my desires,
and the people return to the Uncarved Block.

58

If a government is unobtrusive,
the people become whole.
If a government is repressive,
the people become treacherous.

Good fortune has its roots in disaster,
and disaster lurks with good fortune.
Who knows why these things happen,
or when this cycle will end?
Good things seem to change into bad,
and bad things often turn out for good.
These things have always been hard to comprehend.

Thus the Master makes things change
without interfering.
She is probing yet causes no harm.
Straightforward, yet does not impose her will.
Radiant, and easy on the eye.

59

There is nothing better than moderation
for teaching people or serving Heaven.
Those who use moderation
are already on the path to the Tao.

Those who follow the Tao early
will have an abundance of virtue.
When there is an abundance of virtue,
there is nothing that cannot be done.
Where there is limitless ability,
then the kingdom is within your grasp.
When you know the Mother of the kingdom,
then you will be long enduring.

This is spoken of as the deep root and the firm trunk,
the Way to a long life and great spiritual vision.

60

Governing a large country
is like frying small fish.
Too much poking spoils the meat.

When the Tao is used to govern the world
then evil will lose its power to harm the people.
Not that evil will no longer exist,
but only because it has lost its power.
Just as evil can lose its ability to harm,
the Master shuns the use of violence.

If you give evil nothing to oppose,
then virtue will return by itself.

61

A large country should take the low place like a great watershed,
which from its low position assumes the female role.
The female overcomes the male by the power of her position.
Her tranquility gives rise to her humility.

If a large country takes the low position,
it will be able to influence smaller countries.
If smaller countries take the lower position,
then they can allow themselves to be influenced.
So both seek to take the lower position
in order to influence the other, or be influenced.

Large countries should desire to protect and help the people,
and small countries should desire to serve others.
Both large and small countries benefit greatly from humility.

黃葉詩意圖
衆芳消歇盡楚之客
已闌心復此黃葉落
蕭蕭楓樹林古渡夕陽
亂僧樓夜雨沉記向吴
江别迢迢只到今
舊作并呈
月生先生正 恭壽

62

The Tao is the tabernacle of creation,
it is a treasure for those who are good,
and a place of refuge for those who are not.

How can those who are not good be abandoned?
Words that are beautiful are worth much,
but good behaviour can only be learned by example.

When a new leader takes office,
don't give him gifts and offerings.
These things are not as valuable
as teaching him about the Tao.

Why was the Tao esteemed by the ancient Masters?
Is it not said: 'With it we find without looking.
With it we find forgiveness for our transgressions'?
That is why the world cannot understand it.

暮雲春樹圖
粟香仁兄

63

Act by not acting;
do by not doing.
Enjoy the plain and simple.
Find that greatness in the small.
Take care of difficult problems
while they are still easy;
Do easy things before they become too hard.

Difficult problems are best solved while they are easy.
Great projects are best started while they are small.
The Master never takes on more than she can handle,
which means that she leaves nothing undone.

When an affirmation is given too lightly,
keep your eyes open for trouble ahead.
When something seems too easy,
difficulty is hiding in the details.
The Master expects great difficulty,
so the task is always easier than planned.

64

Things are easier to control while they are quiet.
Things are easier to plan far in advance.
Things break easier while they are still brittle.
Things are easier hid while they are still small.

Prevent problems before they arise.
Take action before things get out of hand.
The tallest tree
begins as a tiny sprout.
The tallest building
starts with one shovel of dirt.
A journey of a thousand miles
starts with a single footstep.

If you rush into action, you will fail.
If you hold on too tight, you will lose your grip.

Therefore the Master lets things take their course
and thus never fails.
She doesn't hold on to things
and never loses them.
By pursuing your goals too relentlessly,
you let them slip away.

If you are as concerned about the outcome
as you are about the beginning,
then it is hard to do things wrong.
The Master seeks no possessions.
She learns by unlearning,
thus she is able to understand all things.
This gives her the ability to help all of creation.

65

The ancient Masters
who understood the way of the Tao,
did not educate people, but made them forget.

Smart people are difficult to guide,
because they think they are too clever.
To use cleverness to rule a country,
is to lead the country to ruin.
To avoid cleverness in ruling a country,
is to lead the country to prosperity.

Knowing the two alternatives is a pattern.
Remaining aware of the pattern is a virtue.
This dark and mysterious virtue is profound.
It is opposite our natural inclination,
but leads to harmony with the heavens.

66

Rivers and seas are rulers
of the streams of hundreds of valleys
because of the power of their low position.

If you want to be the ruler of people,
you must speak to them like you are their servant.
If you want to lead other people,
you must put their interests ahead of your own.

The people will not feel burdened,
if a wise person is in a position of power.
The people will not feel like they are being manipulated,
if a wise person is in front as their leader.
The whole world will ask for her guidance,
and will never get tired of her.
Because she does not like to compete,
no one can compete with the things she accomplishes.

67

The world talks about honouring the Tao,
but you can't tell it from their actions.
Because it is thought of as great,
the world makes light of it.
It seems too easy for anyone to use.

There are three jewels that I cherish:
compassion, moderation, and humility.
With compassion, you will be able to be brave,
With moderation, you will be able to give to others,
With humility, you will be able to become a great leader.
To abandon compassion while seeking to be brave,
or abandoning moderation while being benevolent,
or abandoning humility while seeking to lead
will only lead to greater trouble.
The compassionate warrior will be the winner,
and if compassion is your defence you will be
  secure.
Compassion is the protector of Heaven's salvation.

衡山筆法時在
武進黃山壽寫於四明

68

The best warriors
do not use violence.
The best generals
do not destroy indiscriminately.
The best tacticians
try to avoid confrontation.
The best leaders
become servants of their people.

This is called the virtue of non-competition.
This is called the power to manage others.
This is called attaining harmony with the heavens.

69

There is an old saying:
'It is better to become passive
in order to see what will happen.
It is better to retreat a foot
than to advance only an inch.'

This is called
being flexible while advancing,
pushing back without using force,
and destroying the enemy without engaging him.

There is no greater disaster
than underestimating your enemy.
Underestimating your enemy
means losing your greatest assets.
When equal forces meet in battle,
victory will go to the one
that enters with thc greatest sorrow.

70

My words are easy to understand
and easier to put into practice.
Yet no one in the world seems to understand them,
nor are they able to apply what I teach.

My teachings come from the ancients,
the things I do are done for a reason.

Because you do not know me,
you are not able to understand my teachings.
Because those who know me are few,
my teachings become even more precious.

71

Knowing you don't know is wholeness.
Thinking you know is a disease.
Only by recognizing that you have an illness
can you move to seek a cure.

The Master is whole because
she sees her illnesses and treats them,
and thus is able to remain whole.

72

When people become overly bold,
then disaster will soon arrive.

Do not meddle with people's livelihood;
by respecting them they will in turn respect you.

Therefore, the Master knows herself but is not arrogant.
She loves herself but also loves others.
This is how she is able to make appropriate choices.

73

Being overbold and confident is deadly.
The wise use of caution will keep you alive.

One is the way to death,
and the other is the way to preserve your life.
Who can understand the workings of Heaven?

The Tao of the universe
does not compete, yet wins;
does not speak, yet responds;
does not command, yet is obeyed;
and does not act, but is good at directing.

The nets of Heaven are wide,
but nothing escapes its grasp.

74

If you do not fear death,
then how can it intimidate you?
If you aren't afraid of dying,
there is nothing you cannot do.

Those who harm others
are like inexperienced boys
trying to take the place
of a great lumberjack.
Trying to fill his shoes
will only get them seriously hurt.

75

When people go hungry,
the government's taxes are too high.
When people become rebellious,
the government has become too intrusive.

When people begin to view death lightly,
wealthy people have too much
which causes others to starve.

Only those who do not cling to their life can save it.

76

The living are soft and yielding;
the dead are rigid and stiff.
Living plants are flexible and tender;
the dead are brittle and dry.

Those who are stiff and rigid
are the disciples of death.
Those who are soft and yielding
are the disciples of life.

The rigid and stiff will be broken.
The soft and yielding will overcome.

77

The Tao of Heaven works in the world
like the drawing of a bow.
The top is bent downward;
the bottom is bent up.
The excess is taken from,
and the deficient is given to.

The Tao works to use the excess,
and gives to that which is depleted.
The way of people is to take from the depleted,
and give to those who already have an excess.

Who is able to give to the needy from their excess?
Only someone who is following the way of the Tao.

This is why the Master gives
expecting nothing in return.
She does not dwell on her past accomplishments,
and does not glory in any praise.

78

Water is the softest and most yielding substance.
Yet nothing is better than water,
for overcoming the hard and rigid,
because nothing can compete with it.

Everyone knows that the soft and yielding
overcomes the rigid and hard,
but few can put this knowledge into practice.

Therefore the Master says:
'Only he who is the lowest servant of the kingdom,
is worthy of becoming its ruler.
He who is willing to tackle the most unpleasant tasks,
is the best ruler in the world.'

True sayings seem contradictory.

79

Difficulties remain, even after solving a problem.
How then can we consider that as good?

Therefore the Master
does what she knows is right,
and makes no demands of others.
A virtuous person will do the right thing,
and persons with no virtue will take advantage
of others.

The Tao does not choose sides,
the good person receives from the Tao
because she is on its side.

80

Small countries with few people are best.
Give them all of the things they want,
and they will see that they do not need them.
Teach them that death is a serious thing,
and to be content to never leave their homes.
Even though they have plenty
of horses, wagons and boats,
they won't feel that they need to use them.
Even if they have weapons and shields,
they will keep them out of sight.
Let people enjoy the simple technologies,
let them enjoy their food,
let them make their own clothes,
let them be content with their own homes,
and delight in the customs that they cherish.
Although the next country is close enough
that they can hear their roosters crowing and dogs
barking,
they are content never to visit each other
all of the days of their life.

停琴舉

81

True words do not sound beautiful;
beautiful sounding words are not true.
Wise men don't need to debate;
men who need to debate are not wise.

Wise men are not scholars,
and scholars are not wise.
The Master desires no possessions.
Since the things she does are for the people,
she has more than she needs.
The more she gives to others,
the more she has for herself.

The Tao of Heaven nourishes by not forcing.
The Tao of the Wise Person acts by not competing.

PICTURE CREDITS

Metropolitan Museum of Art, New York: 8, 11, 12, 17, 20, 22, 25, 27, 31, 32, 35, 38, 41, 42, 47, 48, 50, 55, 58, 61, 63, 64, 67, 68, 75, 79, 80, 82, 87, 88, 91, 92, 94, 97, 99, 101, 102, 105, 109, 113, 116, 119, 120, 125, 126

Shutterstock: 14, 18, 28, 36, 45, 52, 57, 70, 73, 76, 84, 106, 110, 114, 122